Road to Independence: United States of America

www.dinobibi.com

Contents

Introduction

When the British colonists in America got tired of Great Britain's rule, they rebelled against it. This period was the American Revolution. During the Revolution, they fought many battles, and the colonies would gradually gain their freedom. Once these colonies gained freedom, they came together to form the independent country of the United States. On the long road to American Independence, the great American Revolutionary War lasted for eight years, from year 1775 until year 1783.

Studying one of the most defining eras in American history is important. The road to independence documented the American Revolution and the rise of the American Republic. These periods are not only important to Americans. Given the influence America has on the world today, it is safe to say these periods are also important to humanity. History shapes the present, and young learners must know about these important periods that formed the land in which they freely live in today.

If people do not understand the critical issues of this road to independence era, they will not be able to come to terms with the events they will later encounter in American history. This book presents historical facts and stories to enable young children gain understanding of this period.

Chapter 1:
The Exodus of Pilgrims from England

In the 18th century, Britons settled in America and formed colonies. The British settlers first made permanent settlement in a city called Jamestown in Virginia. As time went on, these colonies matured and showed behaviors different from their homeland back in Great Britain. They grew in economic strength and cultural expansion. In the 1760s, their combined population increased more than six times their initial population. While they gradually deviated from the traditional British ways of life, they continued to be associated with Britain. In 1763, the British North American colonies demanded separation from Britain, but something happened long before this revolution.

More than a hundred years before, in the year 1620, a ship sailed from Plymouth in England, set for the New Word. The passengers had earlier wanted to sail on a smaller ship called the *Speedwell*, but it could not cope with the high seas. After two failed attempts, they decided to use a different ship. There were 102 passengers on board a ship called the *Mayflower*, which was very large and measured more than 90 feet in height.

Present-day America was not always called America. The region that is now called the United States of America was called the New World back then. Some British settlers had already occupied Virginia, so the sailors of the ship wanted to sail there. The seas were not kind. The stormy weather made the sailors of the *Mayflower* to make mistakes, which resulted in the ship veering off course. Two months later, they arrived in Massachusetts.

The Mayflower

Now, who were these people that travelled so far? Why did they embark on the journey? Out of these 102 passengers on the *Mayflower*, there were 32 people who had been members of the English Separatist Church. They made this journey because they wanted to flee the judgment of the Church of England. They believed the Church of England was corrupt. Years before they fled England, the Church of England had exiled a group of members of their Separatist Church to another European country called Holland. The Separatists did not find Holland favorable, so a man, John Smith, led them to

Virginia. In Virginia, they had founded the first English colony in the year 1607.

During their time in Virginia, the Separatists won the friendship of the London Adventurers, a group of investors whose members were based in London but had other affiliates in York, Hull, Newcastle, and some other parts of England. The Separatists won the trust of the London Adventurers, and as such, they were able to gain financial favors. Thirty of them decided to go back to England. In England, they were able to convince 70 entrepreneurs from the London Adventurers to join their cause.

Mayflower replica

In the year 1620, the 32 Separatists along with the 70 entrepreneurs made up the 102 passengers who boarded the *Mayflower* to go back to Virginia. Unfortunately, they ran into a lot of trouble in the Atlantic Ocean. The turbulent seas threw the Mayflower more than 500 miles of its original course, so it was impossible for them to reach Virginia again. While this was happening, the passengers signed a document called the Mayflower Compact which made sure everyone who signed it would be a member of a civil body politic. The civil body politic established constitutional law and made sure the majority would rule. Thus, the Mayflower Compact was the foundation of the present-day American democracy and politics.

Mayflower Compact Monument, Provincetown, Cape Cod, Massachusetts

After the *Mayflower* veered off course, it took the sailors 66 days before they found land again. They landed on a place called Cape Cod, in a place that is now called Provincetown, Massachusetts.

Shortly after arriving in Provincetown, the ship's captain, a man named Captain Myers Standish, led a group of armed men to go out and look for a more convenient place for them to settle. Soon after they left, while still inside the *Mayflower*, a woman named Susanna White gave birth to a baby boy she named Peregrine. He was the first child to be born to the British settlers.

Pilgrims landing at Plymouth Rock, 1620

Plymouth

On December 21, 1620, the men who had left in search of a better place came back to the ship and reported they would have to stay in Plymouth, just a little distance from Cape Cod. They made Plymouth into a harbor so they could dock the Mayflower. They quickly got to work on making shelters and houses because winter had just started. Winter was difficult for them because they were not adequately prepared. Many of them died of disease. One year later, however, they had become used to their new environment.

Plymouth Rock

By 1621, a year after the Separatists and entrepreneurs had settled, they had elected a governor named Governor William Bradford. During autumn, he invited the neighboring Native American Indians. The natives were the people living in America before the British arrived. He invited the natives because he wanted them to join the settlers in celebrating their first harvest, today known as Thanksgiving. The settlers in Plymouth went ahead to sign treaties with the natives. Soon, the economy grew. As the economy grew, the population grew as well. As the settlers continued to thrive, naturally, many natives began to migrate towards Plymouth. Success naturally attracts people. By the 1640s, there were about 3000 people living in Plymouth.

The first Britons who migrated to America were not initially called pilgrims. People started to refer to the passengers of the *Mayflower* as pilgrims in the 19th century. The 'pilgrim' description originated from a manuscript in which Governor William Bradford had referred to those passengers-settlers as 'saints' who left Holland as 'pilgrims.'

Governor Bradford's House

Chapter 2:
Colonial America

After the pilgrims formed the first colony in Virginia in 1607, as more people continued to migrate to America, they formed 12 more colonies. Many other colonies were formed, but not all of them participated in the American Revolution more than a century later. In the year 1776, these 13 colonies united to form the United States of America.

What is a colony?

A colony is a region under the political and governmental control of another country. The country in control is usually far away from the colony and governs the subordinate country through the aid of officials and vassals. This was the case with England and the 13 colonies. Colonies are formed because migrants travel from the host country, occupy a piece of land, sometimes by conquering the locals, or by merely settling on unoccupied land. In many cases, there may also be settlers from other countries. The American colonies had settlers from Great Britain and other parts of Europe.

Jamestown

Ruins of Jamestown

Jamestown was the first permanent British colony and the first successful British colony in North America. Jamestown is one of the most important pieces of American history, due to its seminal role in the founding of the United States of America. The government, customs, and aspirations of the Jamestown setters are all part of the United States' heritage today.

The Virginia Company of London sponsored Jamestown's establishment. The Virginia Company of London consisted of a group of investors who hoped to profit from establishing Jamestown. King James I chartered the company in 1606.

King James I

Around the time that people left to form Jamestown, the British government was concerned with the growing power of other European nations. It wanted to neutralize the impact of how much these other companies were growing in power and influence, and so it commissioned the Virginia Company of London. The British government tasked the Virginia Company of London with seeking a northwest passage to the Orient which consists of the countries in Eastern Asia. They also had the goal of converting the native Indians to the Anglican religion.

When the British first arrived at Jamestown, they met resistance from both the unfamiliar climate and the native Indians residing in the area. The locals had a powerful chief named Powhatan. The native Indians spoke the Algonquian language and could not communicate with the British. However, they soon found a way to buy and sell with each other. There was also the problem of labor. Many of the original colonists were highborn, so they lacked enough servants and laborers. They were also all men with the first two women arriving at Jamestown a year later, in 1608.

Powhatan

The leader of the colony, Captain John Smith, soon established a "no work, no food" policy. People had to work for their food, or starve. John Smith managed to find ways to trade with the native Indians for food. His rule didn't last long, because in autumn 1609, he was injured by burning gunpowder, so he left for England to seek treatment and never returned. While in England, he continued to promote the colonial expansion of Britain into North America until he died in 1631.

Captain John Smith trading with the Indians

When Smith left, the Virginian settlers suffered. Their relations with the native Indians deteriorated, and they went to war. Many of the colonists died from starvation and disease.

The first slaves arrived in Virginia in the year 1619. The slaves came from a kingdom named Ndongo in Angola. The Portuguese had captured them during invasion and warfare. They were not treated as slaves at first, but as indentured servants, who are people who signed a contract (indenture) and agreed to work for a certain number of years in exchange for transportation to Virginia and food, clothing, and shelter. The practice of slave owning and treatment did not start in America until the late 17th century. When more slaves continued to arrive, they became the primary source of labor in America.

Jamestown was the first representative government, starting in the year 1619 when they convened a general assembly in British America. They convened the general assembly because the settlers wanted to have a say in the laws that governed them. The king of England dissolved the Virginia Company in 1624 after the war with the Powhatan Indians. Some other scandalous events like the misconduct among some of the Virginia Company leaders in England also caused the dissolution. Virginia then became a direct royal colony. Jamestown remained the center of Virginia's political and social life until 1699 when the British government moved the seat of power from Jamestown to Williamsburg. A century later, Jamestown ceased to exist as a town but its significance in the history of the United States of America will never be forgotten.

The Thirteen Colonies

When the British migrated to North America, they hoped to find wealth, establish trade ports, and create new jobs along the coast. Religious leaders or groups looking for religious freedom founded many of the colonies. Other colonies were founded purely for generating new trade opportunities and profits for their investors. Below is a list of the thirteen colonies, who founded them, how they were founded, and in what year they were founded:

1. Virginia (founded in 1607) – by John Smith and the London Adventurers.
2. New York (founded in 1626) – The Dutch originally founded the New York colony, but it became a British colony in the year 1664.
3. New Hampshire (founded in 1623) – John Mason was the first land holder in New Hampshire, but John Wheelwright later made it a colony.
4. Massachusetts Bay (founded in 1630) – Founded by Puritans looking for religious freedom.
5. Maryland (founded in 1633) - George and Cecil Calvert founded Maryland as a safe haven for Catholics.

Cecil Calvert

6. Connecticut (founded in 1636) - Thomas Hooker founded Connecticut after other colonies sent him away from Massachusetts.
7. Rhode Island (founded in 1636) - Roger Williams founded Rhode Island because he wanted to have a place of religious freedom for all.

Roger Williams

8. Delaware (founded in 1638) - Peter Minuit
   and the New Sweden Company founded
   Delaware in 1638 but the British took over it
   and named it a colony in the year 1664.

9. North Carolina (founded in 1663) - Originally part of the Province of Carolina. Split off from South Carolina in 1712.
10. South Carolina (founded in 1663) – South Carolina was originally part of the Province of Carolina, but it split off from North Carolina in the year 1712.
11. New Jersey (founded in 1664) - The Dutch first settled in New Jersey in the year 1664, but the English took over and named it a colony in the year 1664.
12. Pennsylvania (founded in 1681) – by William Penn and the Quakers.

William Penn

13. Georgia (founded in 1732) - James
    Oglethorpe founded Georgia as a place for
    debtors to settle comfortably.

James Oglethorpe

These were not the only colonies in America, nor were they even the largest. With time, as Englishmen continued to establish colonies, there were also plenty of other European migrants coming in droves. The French, Spanish, Dutch, and even Russians migrated to North America and created their colonial outposts on the continent as well. The traditional story of Colonial America is usually restricted to the English colonies that dwelled on the Eastern seaboard of America, but that is an incomplete story. However, the 13 colonies were the ones that led the American Revolution, and that is why they are the most notable colonies when we tell the story today.

During the sixteenth century, that is, the years between 1500 and 1600, England was going through a lot of crisis and confusion. Farmers and landowners realized wool had much more market value than food, so they converted most of the country's farming land to sheep pastures. They forced farmers who were on the lower rungs of the English economical hierarchy to turn in their lands. The result of this trend is that food became scarce because the land was not generating enough food. Also, many farmers lost their jobs. Many people got frustrated and started to leave England for North America.

People also left for America because they found English Christianity too rigid, and they felt they could achieve more religious freedom far away from home. Some rich people took advantage of the rising discontent and sponsored people's journeys from Britain to America. The catch was that they would have to repay their sponsors by working for them. They were under control, in a way, until they could pay off their debts.

In the year 1616, the settlers in Virginia found out how to grow tobacco. Three years later, the first slaves from Africa arrived in Virginia in the year 1619.

By the year 1632, the English government handed over 12 million acres of land at Chesapeake Bay to a man named Cecil Calvert who was the second Lord Baltimore in Maryland. Maryland was a city named after Queen Alexandra Mary Windsor (Queen Elizabeth II). The landowners in Maryland expected this large land and the slaves to generate so much money for the English government. While Maryland resembled Virginia in many ways, Lord Baltimore made sure that unlike Virginia, Maryland would be a colony that offered religious freedom for everyone.

The Pilgrims did not form the 13 colonies in the same way, or at the same time. As Massachusetts continued to expand, people continued to become diverse in their ways of doing things. The settlers could not stay in the same place after some time, so many people had to leave. Different kinds of people came together and went off to form new colonies. Historians typically group the colonies according to their locations on the map and according to the way they were formed. There are three classifications: the New England colonies, the Middle colonies, and the Southern colonies.

The New England Colonies

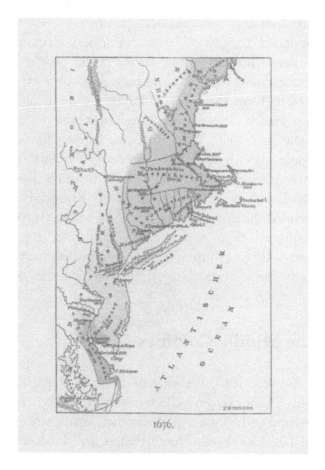

Map of the Massachusetts Bay Colony in 1676

Ten years after the Pilgrims arrived in Plymouth in the year 1620 and found the Plymouth Colony, a wealthy syndicate arose and named itself the

Massachusetts Bay Company. The members sought the help of the locals and learned farming, fishing, and hunting and quickly prospered. As they continued to expand their territories, more new colonies formed. Some conservative people felt Massachusetts was not pious enough, so they left and went to form their own colonies: Connecticut and New Haven. These two colonies later came together in the year 1665. While this was happening, some people also thought Massachusetts was too rigid. These people also left and went to form the Rhode Island colony. The founders of Rhode Island intended the colony to be a colony where everyone who lived there would enjoy complete religious liberty. Also, a group of adventurous settlers travelled north from Massachusetts and formed the New Hampshire colony.

The Middle Colonies

In the year 1664, the king of England at the time, King Charles II, gave the territory in between New England and Virginia to his brother, James, who was the Duke of York. Dutch traders and landowners already occupied the land and called it New Netherland. The landowners and traders were called 'patroons.'

King Charles II

Soon after this hand over, the English took over the Dutch New Netherland and gave it a new name. The new name was New York. While some of the Dutch disagreed with this takeover and left, many of them decided to stay. Some others like the Belgian Flemings and Walloons, French Huguenots, Scandinavians, and Germans living there also stayed back. Because of these events, New York became one of the most culturally diverse and prosperous colonies in the New World.

In the year 1680, the King of England granted 45,000 square miles of land west of the Delaware River to a man named William Penn, a religious man who owned large parcels of land back in Ireland. This handover from the king made Penn very rich. He later founded a colony there and named it after himself. William Penn's named his North American holdings "Penn's Woods," (later renamed to Pennsylvania).

People who knew about William Penn's land soon migrated there. They thought Pennsylvania's soil was fertile and that they would be free to practice whatever religion they had without persecution. Penn wanted to establish his city, so he promised migrants they would have religious freedom. Soon, many more people migrated there from all over Europe.

Most of these emigrants paid their own way to the colonies. They were not servants or slaves, and many of them had enough money to build a life for themselves when they arrived. As a result, Pennsylvania soon prospered as a fair society.

The Southern Colonies

The Southern Colonies originated from Carolina. Named after King Charles I, Carolina was a territory spanning from Virginia all the way down to Florida. Compared to other classes of colonies, Carolina was much less culturally diverse and did not prosper as much. They were not all poor, though. But the wealth was not well distributed. As a result, while people in some parts of Carolina were rich, other people in other parts were very poor. In Northern Carolina, farmers worked hard and earned little. In the south, farmers thrived. They had many large estates in which they produced beef, pork, and corn.

The Southern Carolinians made trade agreements with an English planter colony in Barbados, an island in the Caribbean Sea. The Barbados planter colony settled in the Caribbean to generate revenue for the British Government. The land in Barbados was very fertile, and the weather was favorable. The Barbados planters used a lot of slaves for their plantation work. Due to their ties with Carolina, slave trade thrived between the two colonies. As such, slaves played a huge part in developing the Carolina colony. The Carolina colony later split into two daughter colonies in the year 1729. The two daughter colonies are the present-day North Carolina and South Carolina.

In the year 1732, a man named James Oglethorpe founded Georgia, one of the later colonies. He created the colony because he wanted to release tensions between the British settlers and the Spaniards in Florida. He named the colony Georgia after King George II of England. Georgia developed into a bustling colony in a similar way to how Carolina developed.

Other smaller British colonies in America never became states. These colonies include the Plymouth Colony which later became part of Massachusetts Bay Colony, and the Lost Colony of Roanoke. Other colonies include Newfoundland and Nova Scotia.

Chapter 3:
The French and Indian War

By the beginning of the 18ᵗʰ century, year 1700 to year 1790, about 250,000 people from Europe and Africa settled in North America. 75 years later, that number rose to almost 2.5 million. Several important events, including the French and Indian War (also called the Seven Years' War), the Boston Massacre, the Boston Tea Party, the Continental Congress, and the Revolutionary War led to the eventual American Revolution.

The French and Indian War marked a phase in which France and Great Britain went to war for nine years. A more complicated war, The Seven Years' War, happened within the French and Indian War. These wars determined who would later control the colonies in North America.

What Caused the French and Indian War?

The major reason for the French and Indian War was a dispute over whether the upper Ohio River was part of the British Empire or the French. If it was under British, then the Virginians and Pennsylvanians would be able to settle there and trade. If it was part of the French, then it would be under France's control. The two nations could not come to an agreement, and so the conflict snowballed.

There was also another problem. Which national culture would be the backbone of North America? The British argued that, since they were the ones who first settled in the regions in which they mostly occupied, they should have cultural and governmental control. France argued that they should have the whole Mississippi Valley and its surrounding areas.

These conflicts did not arise in isolation. They had their roots in earlier history. The pilgrims were not the first Europeans to land in North America. Back in the 15th century, a man named John Cabot explored the North American continent. In the 17th century, when the British colonies were expanding, an English royal charter granted all the lands between the Atlantic Ocean and the Pacific Ocean to the Virginia Company and Plymouth Company. They amended the charter two years later. The new territory would include the North Carolina, South Carolina, and Georgia colonies. All lands between the border of the French-held colony and the Spanish-held Florida would belong to England.

Italian explorer John Cabot reaches Labrador in Canada, 1497

For the French, a man named René-Robert Cavelier, Sieur de la Salle sailed from Canada in 1682 and moved through the Great Lakes. As he sailed down from the Mississippi River in 1682, he took possession of the lands around it and its tributaries in name of the King of France.

Robert de La Salle exploring the coast of Louisiana

For 60 years, the two countries argued over which country had the stronger claim to the lands in the great Mississippi basin. The Englishmen gradually settled all along the Atlantic seaboard to the south of the Gulf of Saint Lawrence. In Saint Lawrence, more colonies flourished. These newer colonies included the British colony of Nova Scotia which was founded in 1749. Soon enough, the people who lived in these colonies grew west from the tidal areas and established themselves in the Piedmont country.

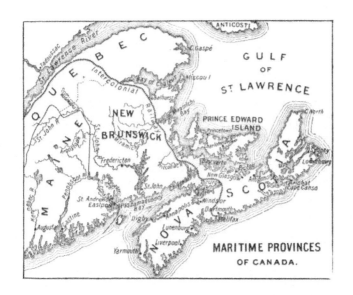

Gulf of St. Lawrence and Nova Scotia

Towards the mid-18th century, the Virginians spread so much that there were small Virginian houses and huts all the way west of the Appalachians. By then, Pennsylvanian traders had settled among the Indian people who dwelled in the upper Ohio Valley and were British allies. The French, on the other hand, who had held colonial and territorial control of Canada from the early 17th century, gradually expanded into the Great Lakes region. As they kept expanding, the French settled permanently in Detroit.

As the conflict dragged on, the French governor-general ordered a man named Joseph Celeron de Blainville to make sure all the trading houses on the Allegheny River and upper Ohio River lowered the British flags that flew over them. The French labeled the British traders as trespassers on French lands. This action forced the British traders to flee back to the eastern Appalachian slopes. In 1752, the French used force and provoked war. They destroyed the British colonial trading center at Pickawillany, a town on the upper Great Miami River. They captured and killed every trader who spoke English.

When the residents in Ohio heard that the French were capturing and killing Englishmen, Lt. Gov. Robert Dinwiddie decided to retaliate. In the year 1753, during fall, he sent out a very young George Washington to the fort of the French people, a place called Fort LeBoeuf. Washington went to Fort LeBoeuf to warn the French soldiers there that they were trespassing. He claimed the land that they occupied belonged to Virginia. Virginia was under British rule. They ignored his warnings.

Washington sent word back to Virginia that the French did not want to give up the land. Virginia allied with the Ohio Company and raised money to build a fort at the spot where River Allegheny and River Monongahela joined together. (River Monongahela is the river that we call Pittsburgh River today.)

George Washington crossing the Alleghany River, 1753

In spring, while the Virginians were still building the fort, the French army came down River Allegheny and took over the building project. They tore the place down before the British soldiers could arrive. When the commander of the British militia (a group of regular citizens who support the regular army when there is an emergency), a man named Col. Joshua Fry, died, Washington assumed command of the militia and assembled a larger militia at Fort Necessity, what we now call Confluence, Pennsylvania. By this time, the French soldiers had camped at Fort Duquesne. The two forts were only 40 miles away from each other.

On May 28, 1754, Washington's militia captured the members of a small French scouting group consisting of 30 armed men. They killed the commander, Coulon de Jumonville, and nine other soldiers, and took the remaining captives. The French forces were angry and retaliated.

The French attacked Fort Necessity on July 3 of the same year. They allied with Indians and attacked the base ruthlessly. Although, Washington had fortified his forces and strengthened his militia, his forces were still no match for the combined power of the French and the Indians. Washington surrendered and fled with his men back to Virginia. The French burned Fort Necessity down.

After their defeat at Fort Necessity, the Virginians begged London for help. King George II did not accept their request at first because he did not want to go to full-scale war with France again. His prime minister, the duke of Newcastle, asked him to 'Let Americans fight Americans.' King George II's government observed for a while, but soon noticed the Virginians would not survive on their own. He sent General Edward Braddock to Virginia with the mission to force the French out of Fort Duquesne and the surroundings. The King of England also sent the navy to America. Admiral Edward Boscawen led the British Navy. His mission was to block the seas and prevent the French from calling for reinforcements to Canada. The British were officially at war with the French and the Indians.

King George II

For the first four years, the French overwhelmed the British forces. They killed General Braddock in battle, and the survivors from the British army fled helter-skelter. The French ambushed General

46

Braddock's army, and other army leaders surrendered. Fort Oswego, Fort William Henry, and Fort Louisburg all surrendered to the French. Even when General James Abercrombie attacked the French force at Lake George with a superior army, he faced a resounding defeat. Almost all his men died in battle. The English settlers who occupied the areas that are now central New York, western Maryland, and central Pennsylvania ran away. Thousands of families fled east to escape the wrath of the French soldiers.

Death of General Braddock

While all these were going on in North America, back in England, a man named William Pitt did something remarkable. His political opponents and enemies had sidelined him, but the losing efforts of the British army in America gave him an opportunity. He figured that even though the battle between the British and the French and Indians had spread to other parts of the world, he could still turn things around for his people. He took over the British war effort and recruited new soldiers to reinforce the depleted parts of the British army.

William Pitt

William Pitt pleaded with the British Parliament to give him as much money as possible. He left no stone unturned in inspecting details of the operations in North America. He could not allow anything to go to chance, to prevent another losing streak. From this moment on, William Pitt oversaw the British victory in North America.

While William Pitt was rebuilding the British forces, the British Royal Navy was also improving in its efforts to subdue the French. The Navy slowly overpowered the French ships at sea. They attacked and defeated every ship they came across. They subdued warships, merchant shops, and warships alike. They prevented the French from reinforcing their troops in North America. Nothing could enter Canada from France. Admiral Jean-François de la Clue-Sabran failed to force a section of the French fleet into Canada in August 1759. The British Royal Navy led by Admiral Edward Boscawen destroyed his fleet at Lagos, Portugal. Later in the same year, the French completely lost the naval war to the British. The commander of the British Naval forces, a man named Admiral Edward Hawke, cut down the French navy to pieces in the battle of Quiberon Bay.

During this time, France was undergoing national bankruptcy, and their economy was in shambles. They could not continue the war. Britain, on the other hand, had a lot of money to spend. The British economy was growing stronger. The British colonies in America also had plenty of food, while the French Canadians suffered famine due to the British Navy placing blockades off the coast of France and in the

Gulf of St. Lawrence. It was impossible for the French to import food.

The Treaty of Paris

When the French could not cope in the war anymore, they decided to appeal for a peace treaty. They signed the peace Treaty of Paris in February 10, 1763. The terms of the treaty stated that France was to vacate Canada and hand over authority to Great Britain. They were also to surrender their claims to the River Mississippi and its surrounding areas, Louisiana, and New Orleans.

During the last days of the war, Spain tried to stop the British from acquiring lands in the Caribbean, but failed woefully. Due to their failure, they had to give up Florida to get Havana. The Spanish would, however, get Louisiana and New Orleans from France. By this treaty, the French were giving up their power in every part of North America. The British effectively held all the power in North America, unopposed. They had power all the way from the ends of the Hudson Bay down to the Florida Keys.

One would think that, since the British forces helped the American colonies win their wars against France, the Americans would pledge loyalty to the British

Empire forever. Ironically, however, that very victory made the Americans distrustful of the British.

Before the French and Indian War, the Americans held their connections to the British Empire very highly. After the war, however, the Americans did not want to continue depending on the British for help all the time. They felt that if the British crown kept on coming to their aid, they would keep demanding huge obligations from them.

With all their enemies wiped out from the continent, the Americans grew bold. They started to question the authority the British crown had over them. When the British crown imposed taxes on them, the Americans revolted. These conflicts set the pace for the American Revolution in the next coming years.

The Stamp Act and the Townsend Acts

The British crown imposed the Stamp Act on America to increase revenue to expand and defend the rapidly growing British Empire. This was the first time the British Parliament tried to directly impose taxes on the Americans. They imposed taxes on everything, from newspaper advertisements to ships' bills of landing. The Americans revolted and discarded the Stamp Act. They refused to use the stamps. They rioted, they burned stamps, and they intimidated the stamp distributors.

After the Stamp Act, the British enacted four acts. In these acts, the British Parliament tried to enforce its historic right to have authority over colonial America. They suspended the American assembly because they thought it was stubborn for no reason. These acts were the Townsend Acts. These Townsend Acts drew the ire of the Americans who resisted them. The Americans verbally boycotted the Townsend Acts. They resorted to physical violence. They fought British agents and went on strikes. They also refused to do business with British traders. The British government responded in October 1768 by sending two British Army regiments to America. These regiments landed in Boston, Massachusetts.

Chapter 4:
The Boston Massacre and Boston Tea Party

The Boston Massacre

Site of the Boston Massacre in Massachusetts

The Boston Massacre happened on March 5, 1770. The massacre was a fight between British soldiers and a crowd in Boston. This incident was one of the most significant events that made the Americans hate the British more and inspired the American Revolution.

Three years earlier, in the year 1767, the British tried to regain the funds they had invested in defending the North American colonies. Their investments had won the colonies the war, so the British Parliament felt entitled to American loyalty. The Parliament imposed heavy taxes and strict revenue collection through the Townsend Acts from the colonies to recoup their investment. The Parliament also imposed the Townsend Acts to enforce their authority over the colonies. These moves by the British Parliament angered the Americans. The Americans revolted by boycotting the British and harassing their officials. Seeing that their hold over America was threatened, the British government dispatched two regiments to Boston.

When the British regiments arrived in Boston the next year, the Americans became very distrustful of the British. In 1770, some Americans boycotted the British, but some Americans continued to do business with the British. The Americans who boycotted the British became angry at the ones who were still doing business with them.

Radical boycotters, known as the Sons of Liberty, made signposts and hoisted them on the establishments of those merchants who did not boycott and insulted their customers. The Sons of Liberty was an organization that arose in the American colonies in 1765 to oppose the Stamp Act.

On February 22, a man named Ebenezer Richardson, the radicals knew as an informer, tried to take down one of those signposts from his neighbor, Theophilus Lillie's, shop. When Richardson tried to take the signpost down, a group of boys attacked him. They drove Richardson back into his own home. When Richardson ran into his home and shut the door, he came back out to insult the boys. They hurled stones that broke his door and front window. A man named George Wilmot joined Richardson, and they both grabbed muskets (a muzzle-loaded long gun) and attacked the boys who had, by this time, entered Richardson's backyard.

Richardson fired and hit an 11-year-old boy, Christopher Seider, who died from his wounds later that night. The chaos drew a huge crowd that was ready to attack Richardson. They did not, however, as they expected Richardson would be brought to justice in court.

The city was filled with tension which soon escalated to fights between soldiers and rope makers in southern Boston. On March 4, British soldiers searched a factory owned by a man named John Gray. The soldiers then planned to attack Gray's workers the next day. When Gray heard of the plan, he sought Colonel William Dalrymple's help. Colonel Dalrymple was the commander of one of the regiments the Parliament had dispatched to America the year before. The Colonel agreed that he was going to command his men to stand down if Gray did the same to his men.

The next morning, someone posted a handbill declaring that the British were ready to defend themselves at all cost. By nightfall, Bostonians filled the streets. Rumors were flying around that the soldiers intended to cut down an elm tree in southern Boston. The elm tree was significant because it was the tree were men met to discuss protesting the Stamp Act. They had written "The Tree of Liberty" on a sign and hung it on the tree. Rumors also flew that a soldier had killed a man who sold oysters.

The crowd attacked the barracks of one of the British Regiments but was repelled. Some people rung alarm bells, and the crowd doubled. The soldiers of the Regiment, however, stayed indoors in the barracks. The crowd became angrier and angrier, and they threw rocks and snowballs at the barrack's gates.

When the soldiers continued ignoring them, the crowd directed their anger on a sentry, soldier who stands outside to keep guard, who stood outside the Customs House. About 50 or 60 people threatened to attack the sentry. When a man named Captain Thomas Preston heard of the sentry's condition, he sent out seven soldiers armed with bayonets to rescue the sentry. A bayonet is a knife, sword, or spike-shaped weapon that fits on the end of a gun, so it can function as a spear.

The crowd knew the soldiers were not allowed to open fire on them, as the riot act had not been read yet, so they took advantage of it. They also knew that even though they read the Riot Act, the soldiers could only shoot at them if they failed to disperse within the hour. The crowd made jest of the soldiers and hurled them with any object they could lay their hands on. They threw stones, sticks, ice, snowballs, and oyster shells at the soldiers.

While all this was going on, the crowd trapped one of the soldiers near the Customs House and threw him around. The soldier panicked and mistakenly fired his gun. The other soldiers thought the shot they heard was the order to shoot, so they discharged their weapons. The shots hit three men who died instantly. One of the men, Crispus Attucks, was black former slave. These three men were not the only men hit; the gunfire hit eight other people. Two of these other eight people died later that day.

While the chaos was going on, Lieutenant Governor Thomas Hutchinson arrived at the scene and tried to prevent the violence from escalating further. He ordered Captain Thomas Preston to take his men back into the barracks. Lieutenant Governor

Hutchinson then went back to the Old State House and promised the crowd that justice would be done. Doing so, Hutchinson restored an uneasy calmness to the city.

Lieutenant Governor Thomas Hutchinson

The next morning, the Bostonian government arrested Captain Thomas Preston and the seven soldiers he had commanded to go out into the crowd. They also arrested the sentry who the men had tried to rescue. They called a town meeting. The town meeting demanded that the British remove all their troops. By March 11, both regiments decamped from the barracks and went back to Castle William (a place renamed as Castle Island) in the Boston Harbor.

The British customs commissioners who were in town also left because they were afraid for their safety. While this was going on, both the British and the Americans tried to prove to the public that the other side was the cause of the problem. A journalist named Benjamin Edes described the incident as 'a horrid massacre.'

Boston Massacre

Colonel Dalrymple got 31 people to testify and then compiled a report which he titled 'A Fair Account of the Late Unhappy Disturbance at Boston in New England.' James Bowdoin, Samuel Pemberton, and Joseph Warren, on the other hand, got 86 people to testify. The 96 respondents described the event as murder and circulated their reports in pamphlets across town. Colonel Preston, who was in jail at the time, wrote his own side of the event which he titled 'Case of Capt. Thomas Preston.' The only thing in common with all these accounts was that they all told stories of the events of the Boston Massacre, though the stories were all different.

James Forrest, a man who sided with the British, was Captain Preston's friend. He asked his friend, a man named Josiah Quincy, Jr. to represent Captain Preston and his men during trial. Josiah Quincy, Jr. and his colleague, Robert Auchmuty, Jr. agreed to defend the soldiers only if they would let a man named John Adams be part of the defense team. The man, John Adams, would later become the second President of the United States of America. No one really knows why he agreed to take the case, but it may have been because he believed that everyone deserves a fair trial. Therefore, defense team constituted Josiah Quincy, Jr., Robert Auchmuty, Jr., and John Adams. On the other hand, Josiah Quincy, Jr.'s brother, Samuel Quincy, was going to be the prosecutor.

John Adams

The defense team believed it was easier to save Captain Preston and his men by separating the trials. They obtained one trial for Captain Preston and then another for his men. They soon realized the trial had a bigger agenda than just determining justice. There were political agendas layered in the case. The defense was trying to prove that the Sons of Liberty were dangerous to the land as a mob, while the prosecution was trying to condemn the British Parliament's forceful attempt to suppress the colonists' political rights.

While the case dragged on, John Adams argued that there was no way to prove who had commanded the men to fire or if there was a command at all. He managed to convince the court that the soldiers did not intend to cause a riot, as they were only acting out of fear. He was able to win the case for Captain Preston and his men. However, the court demanded that two of Captain's men be punished. John Adams argued further that the only crime they could be accused of was involuntary murder. He was able to reduce their charges to manslaughter. He then invoked a part of an old English law called 'plea to clergy.' According to the plea of clergy, the convicted people could only have their thumbs branded as first-time offenders. The outcome of this trial was how those soldiers escaped harsh judgment.

The Boston Tea Party

The Boston Tea Party

In 1773, some Bostonians disguised themselves as Mohawk people and dumped about £18,000 worth of tea into the harbor in the event we now call The Boston Tea Party.

The East India Company was becoming increasingly powerful when it started running into financial problems. It begged the British government to grant it a monopoly on all tea exported to America. The British government accepted, and then went ahead to also permit the Company to bypass colonial wholesalers and supply retailers directly.

At this time, almost all the tea the colonists were enjoying was illegal and tax free. The monopoly would make smuggling tea unprofitable. The East India Company wanted to sell tea at a much cheaper price than the customary one, thereby putting the colonial merchants out of business. The colonial traders then joined the radicals to agitate for independence.

On December 16, 1773, under the cover of darkness, Samuel Adams, who was John Adams' brother, led a group of Boston men who disguised themselves as Mohawk Indians and boarded three anchored British ships and dumped their tea cargo into Boston Harbor. They feared fellow colonists would buy the tea and pay tax for it if the tea ever landed.

Samuel Adams

The East India Company then responded by threatening that if the Boston Tea Party went unpunished, it would tell the world that Britain had lost control over its colonies. The British publicly condemned the Boston Tea Party. They branded it an act of vandalism and called for legal measures to bring the culprits to order.

The British Parliament eventually passed a series of punishments called the Intolerable Acts, which shut off Boston's sea trade until they repaid the cost of the destroyed tea. While the British thought they had the Bostonians under control, ironically, the British Parliament's attempt at targeting Massachusetts only united the colonies even more towards the Revolution.

War was coming.

Continental Congress

The Continental Congress refers to the body of delegates who represented the people of the colonies and made decisions on behalf of them. After the Boston Port closed during the Intolerable Acts, the colonies began to dislike each other. During spring in the year 1774, the first Continental Congress was held to find a solution to the Acts. They all elected and agreed that a man named Peyton Randolph would be the President of the Continental Congress. They also elected Charles Thomson of Pennsylvania to be the Secretary of the Congress.

Congress Hall in Philadelphia

To make sure that the process was fair, they decided that every state would have one vote no matter how big or small it was. They chose the first Continental Congressmen thus: Patrick Henry, George Washington, John Adams and his brother, Sam Adams, and John Dickinson. These men met in secret to decide the colonists' response to the British rule. They rejected the plan to join British authority with colonial freedom. They decided, instead, that they would focus on declaring personal rights which included rights to life, property, liberty, assembly, as well as right to trial by jury. They also rejected British taxes and the British army. They, however, accepted that the British Parliament could regulate their commerce.

They decided they would hold a second Congress to determine whether they would boycott British goods and cease to do business with Britain and the West Indies. Before the second Congress could hold, however, problem arose in Massachusetts. The Congress accepted new members. The new member included Thomas Jefferson and Benjamin Franklin. The Congress gradually cut ties with Britain until there was nothing left to cut.

On July 2, 1776, the Continental Congress proclaimed the United Colonies will from henceforth be free and independent states. Only New York stayed out of this decision. Two days later, the Continental Congress solemnly approved this statement, which later came to be known as the Declaration of Independence. The Continental Congress also prepared a series of articles called the Articles of Confederation. After all the states approved the Articles of Confederation, in March 1781, they were proclaimed as the first U.S.

Constitution. More about the Declaration of Independence in chapter 7.

Signing of the Declaration of Independence

Chapter 5:
Revolutionary War

War did not start right away, but everyone knew war was coming.

In the year 1774, some colonies formed armed militias made up of people called 'minutemen.' The British heard about it and sent General Thomas Gage to neutralize them. General Gage raided their stores and seized their weapons and ammunitions. Some people who named themselves patriots were extremely loyal to the colonial government. They reported the incident with General Gage to the colonial governments. In December of the same year, the patriots raided Fort William and Mary at New Hampshire and seized a large amount of gunpowder belonging to the British forces.

Minuteman statue in Concord, New Hampshire

The British had been targeting Massachusetts, especially Boston, for a long time now, and so they promptly declared Massachusetts a rogue state in open rebellion. The British Parliament gave General Gage the authority to use as much force as possible to take over the state. When the patriot spies led by Paul Revere and William Dawes heard of the order, they mounted their horses and rode back to Lexington to warn the minutemen of the impending attack. The next day, both forces met in battle at the Battles of Lexington and Concord.

The Battles of Lexington and Concord

Battles of Lexington and Concord

Very early in the morning of the next day, Lieutenant Colonel Francis Smith and Major John Pitcairn arrived in Lexington with the British forces. Pitcairn demanded that the colonial militia lay down their arms and flee. As the militia began to disperse, a shot rang out from nowhere. This shot was called the shot 'that was heard round the world.' After the initial shock, both sides exchanged fire. The British army charged forward and drove the militia from the grassy field. After a while, when things calmed down a bit, eight of the militiamen lay dead and another ten were wounded. One British soldier sustained an injury.

Later, the British pursued the militiamen towards Concord, but other towns reinforced the colonial militia by sending more men. Colonel James Barrett led his men to attack the British but could not defeat them. In the end, the colonial militia was forced to run back to Concord. The British army led by Smith continued to pursue the militiamen to Boston when the militia started running towards the sea.

More militia men poured out of the towns to join the fighting. Lieutenant Colonel Francis Smith realized the colonists were gaining advantage, so he ordered his men to form a flank column to protect the main force. One mile from Concord, the colonist militia seized the opportunity and launched several attacks.

The British started to retreat towards Lexington. As they got close Lexington, Captain John Parker's militiamen ambushed them. They waited until they saw Lt. Col. Smith before opening fire. The British soldiers managed to get to Lexington. They were tired and most of them were injured from their march, so they were glad to find out that they had had reinforcements brought in by Hugh and Earl Percy. Earl Percy waited for Lt. Col. Smith's men to rest a bit before resuming the march back to Boston. Brigadier General William Heath had assumed command of the colonist militia by this time. Heath decided to keep the British surrounded with a loose ring of militia for the remainder of the march to ensure maximum damage. This way, the militia kept firing into the British column from a safe distance until they got to Charlestown.

There were a lot of casualties on both sides of the battles. The colonist militia of Massachusetts recorded 50 dead men, 39 wounded, and 5 missing soldiers. The British lost 73 men, reported 173 wounded soldiers, and 26 men were missing. These battles, Lexington and Concord, became the first major battles of the American Revolution. Soon enough, other colonies sent more men to the Massachusetts militia until they had a force of about 20,000 soldiers. These men later fought the Battle of Bunker Hill.

The Battle of Bunker Hill

The Battle of Bunker Hill

The Battle of Bunker Hill was the first major battle in the American Revolutionary War. The battle took place in Charlestown. If you go to Charlestown today, you can visit the Bunker Hill Monument. It is a 67-meter tall obelisk made of granite that marks the site where the bloody battle took place. The British forces won the battle, but they won it at great cost. They lost a lot in the battle, so much that the victory felt bitter. The colonists lost, but the events of the battle gave them hope.

Bunker Hill monument

Two months after the Battles of Lexington and Concord, the colonies of Massachusetts, New Hampshire, Rhode Island, and Connecticut assembled an army of about 15,000 soldiers. The troops intended to attack the British army which numbered just about 5,000. The commander-in-chief of the colonial army was a man named General Artemas Ward. He realized his army was vulnerable to any attack from Dorchester Heights, Bunker Hill, and Breed Hill. When he heard that the British army was heading towards Dorchester Heights, he attempted to fortify the hill.

The British commander, General Thomas Gage, sent out 2,300 soldiers to attack the colonists. He gave Major General William Howe command over these men. When his men got close to Dorchester Heights, the British gave them heavy gunfire. The British attacked and defeated the colonists. The colonists had been firing for hours and were tired. All that time, the British just hid behind rail fences and waited it out before they launched their attack. About 450 colonists and 1,000 British lost their lives in that battle. Many on both sides sustained serious injuries.

The British soldiers could have finished the colonists off, but they had suffered heavy damage to their troops, and so they went away. The colonists, on the other hand, did not back down even though more of their men died. The tenacity of the colonists even in the fate of adversity discouraged the British, so the British abandoned the battle.

Two weeks later, George Washington (who was now a general) became the commander of the colonists' army.

The Siege of Boston

Since the Battles of Lexington and Concord ended, the colonists laid siege to Boston. They were tired of the British taking over their city, so 15,000 untrained men came together to form an army. They called themselves the Continental Army. They surrounded Boston. The British forces, led by Thomas Gage, who occupied the city numbered about 6,500 men.

After the Battle of Bunker Hill, General William Howe took over command of the British army from General Gage. George Washington was the commander of the colonist army. Both armies fought each other in small battles for months without a winner. The next year, General Washington assembled an army and marched to Dorchester Heights to send the British away. This act, plus the events of the Battle of Bunker Hill encouraged the colonists. The fact that the inexperienced colonists could inflict such damage on the more skilled British army made them believe in themselves.

William Howe

The Treaty of Paris

The Treaty of Paris, not to be confused with the Treaty of Paris of 1763, ended the America Revolutionary War. On November, 30, 1782, both American and British governments made the first attempt to end the Revolutionary War. Ten months later, they sorted out their problems and agreed on the treaty. They named it Treaty of Paris because they signed the treaty in Paris, France. Once they signed the treaty, the war ended. From then on, America was an independent country.

Chapter 6:
The First Presidency

George Washington

George Washington had served as Commander-in-Chief of the Continental Army during the American

Revolutionary War. He had been very instrumental in America's victory and independence. He had also been the President of the 1787 Constitutional Convention where a stable and suitable Constitution of the United States of America was created. It was no surprise that the general public loved and respected him greatly. They expected him to become the first president of the United States of America once the Constitution was approved. However, he had been a public servant for a long time, and he wanted to retire to his fields. Several politicians rose to persuade him because he was the only one that could unite the new country. Washington did not think he was experienced enough to lead the country, but he eventually accepted to run.

The outcome of the election showed just how much the public believed in him. He had 69 electoral votes. John Adams received 34 electoral votes and 10 other candidates split 35 electoral votes. By the law that applied then, all candidates ran for presidency. The candidate who then had the most electoral votes became president and the second-place candidate became vice-president.

On April 30, 1789, Washington was sworn in as the first President of the United States of America. In no time, he got to work. The first 100 days of his presidency were marked with tireless and fruitful activity. He signed the Judiciary Act of 1789, which established the federal court system in the United States. During his presidency, Washington appointed three chief justices and eight associate justices to the Supreme Court. He supervised the establishment of the new federal government and appointed all the high-ranking officials in the executive branch.

Modern day Supreme Court building

Also during his first term in office, Washington signed the country's first copyright law and created the U.S. Postal Service. He established the first national bank which dealt with the debt incurred from the American Revolution. He shaped numerous political practices, such as the social life of the President. He also established the site of the permanent capital of the United States which is named after him as Washington D.C.

He supported the economic policies proposed by Finance Minister, Alexander Hamilton, whereby the federal government took on the debts of the state governments. He established the United States Mint and the United States Customs Service. In his tenure as president, Congress approved taxes to pay for the government's expenses and help the country mature economically.

Alexander Hamilton

Washington did not feel it was below him to personally lead federal soldiers to suppress the Whiskey Rebellion. The Whiskey Rebellion was a protest that the citizens made against taxes in his administration. He directed the Northwest Indian War. A result of this was that the United States gained control over Native American tribes in the Northwest Territory.

In foreign affairs, his wise decisions maintained domestic peace. He issued the 1793 Proclamation of Neutrality which kept America out of the raging French Revolutionary War by the European powers. He also negotiated two important treaties, the 1794 Jay Treaty with Great Britain and the 1795 Treaty of San Lorenzo with Spain. Both treaties advanced trade and helped the country gain control of its frontier. To protect American shipping from Barbary pirates and other threats, he re-established the United States Navy with the Naval Act of 1794.

Mount Vernon

Understanding that his actions in office would dictate the actions of numerous presidents after him, he voluntarily left office after two terms of four years each. After Washington resigned from the presidency on March 4, 1797, he returned to his home. He died on December 14, 1799, from a throat infection at his home in Mount Vernon.

Chapter 7:
Important Documents

Thomas Paine's *Common Sense* Pamphlets

Even after the bloody battles of Lexington, Concord, and Bunker Hill, things were still difficult in Colonial America. Instead of an all-out war between two countries, it seemed more like a civil war. Things went on like that until a man named Thomas Paine published a pamphlet and named it *Common Sense*. The warring factions had been avoiding the topic, but *Common Sense* made the seeds of independence take root in people's minds.

Thomas Paine's *Common Sense* pamphlet, published in 1776 at the beginning of the revolution, was 50 pages long and sold 100, 000 copies in just a few months! This *Common Sense* pamphlet was the turning point in the events leading to the Declaration of Independence.

The Declaration of Independence

Before, during, and after the Battles of Lexington and Concord, the colonists demanded their rights within the British Empire. They did not really want to separate from the British Empire. They were fine with British rule, but when the British started making all those demands and bringing all those soldiers, the colonists started to get restless. They demanded their rights to independent rule. As the battles progressed, the colonists wanted independence more.

In April 1776, North Carolina ordered their representatives in Congress to vote for independence. The next month, the Virginian colony ordered its deputy members to propose a motion. This motion stated that 'United Colonies are, and of right ought to be, free and independent states.' A congressman named Richard Henry Lee brought presented the motion to Congress. John Adams seconded the motion.

Declaration of Independence

The Congress approved the Declaration of Independence because they wanted every American to have rights to life, liberty, and happiness. The Declaration of Independence would protect these rights. The Declaration of Independence made sure the people would choose their government, and then the government would rule with the permission of the people. The Declaration of Independence also provided that the people have the duty to change the government.

Congress denied British parliamentary rule and cut ties with the British government. In May 1776, Congress asked the colonies to form their own governments. Congress also advised the colonies not to pledge in any way to the British.

Some colonies initially hesitated, so the motion was delayed. A man named John Dickinson argued that they should first form a central government and try to gain help from foreign countries before declaring independence. The Congress, however, went ahead to ask the committee to work on a statement to claim independence officially. On July 1, the Congress met to vote on the motion. Nine colonies voted for independence and complete separation from the British Empire. Even though John Dickinson opposed the motion, the rest of Congress voted in support. The next day, the Congress met at the Pennsylvania State House and approved the vote results. The Pennsylvania State House is now known as Independence Hall. New York did not vote on that day because the representatives from New York had not received permission to vote. New York later voted in favor of the motion two weeks later, on July 15, 1776.

John Dickinson

On July 19, the Congress approved the document the committee had prepared and named it "The Unanimous Declaration of the Thirteen United States of America." Timothy Matlack of Philadelphia officially wrote it down on parchment and filed it for public recording. Members of the Congress signed the parchment on August 2, while some others signed later.

Independence Hall

Thomas Jefferson wrote the first draft of the Declaration of Independence and edited it with the members of his committee. The Declaration of Independence is one of the most valuable pieces of modern history. It inspired several countries over the years. The Declaration of Independence is important because it contained the first formal declaration by a nation. By the Declaration, Americans demanded their right to have a government of their own choice.

Thomas Jefferson

Chapter 8:
The United States Bill of Rights

The first 10 amendments that the United States government made to the United States Constitution were called the Bill of Rights. The reason for the amendments was to make sure that people would not lose their freedom. The Bill of Rights would limit the power and control the government had over the people. The Bill of Rights made provisions for the freedom of religion, speech, right to bear weapons, rights to form organizations, and others.

The idea for the Bill of Rights came about when many colonial representatives refused to sign the Constitution without some adjustments. A man, James Madison, wrote 12 amendments to the Constitution and presented them to the Congress in the year 1789. In 1791, the Congress accepted 10 of these amendments. Congress later called these 10 amendments the Bill of Rights.

James Madison

The 10 amendments are still valid today. The 10
amendments which made up the Bill of Rights are:

1. The First Amendment says Congress will not make any law that promotes any religion or forbids it. This amendment also protects the citizens' freedom of speech, freedom of assembly, freedom of the press, and the right to petition the government when they are unhappy with its rule.
2. The Second Amendment says that citizens can bear arms.
3. The Third Amendment makes sure that the government cannot place soldiers in private homes.
4. The Fourth Amendment restricts the government from searching and seizing the property of Americans without reason. The government get a warrant from a judge before they can do search a citizen's home.
5. The Fifth Amendment is the reason while people usually say 'I take the Fifth' during a trial. Because of the Fifth Amendment, people can decide not to testify in court if they feel that their testimony may put them into trouble. The Fifth Amendment does not end there. It also protects citizens from criminal prosecution and punishment without due process. Also, because of the Fifth Amendment, people cannot be tried in court for the same crime more than once. Finally, the Fifth Amendment also makes it possible that the government cannot seize private

property for public use without fair compensation.

6. The Sixth Amendment makes a quick trial by a jury of one's peers possible. If the government or anyone accuses another person or people of a crime, the accused must be told the exact crimes. They can also challenge the witnesses. The Sixth Amendment also makes sure the accused person or people must have legal representation (this means that the government has to provide a lawyer if the accused cannot afford one).

7. The Seventh Amendment makes it possible for civil cases to be tried by jury.

8. The Eight Amendment says no to excessive bail, exorbitant fines, and cruel punishments.

9. The Ninth Amendment states that the list of constitutional rights is not complete, and that the people still have more rights that may not be on the list.

10. The Tenth Amendment declares that all powers that the United States government don't have in the Constitution are for individuals or for the state.

Chapter 9:
John Adams Presidency

On March 4, 1797, John Adams was sworn in as the second President of the United States of America. His tenure ended after one term on March 4, 1801, when he lost to his vice president, Thomas Jefferson. Adams had served as vice president under George Washington from 1789 to 1797. But before then, he had always been a leader of the American Revolution.

After Adams left Harvard College, he went on to become one of the best attorneys in Boston. Not only was he intelligent, he was patriotic and opinionated. During the 1760s, Adams began to challenge Great Britain's authority in colonial America. He saw the British imposition of high taxes and tariffs as a tool of oppression. He no longer believed the actions of the English government had the colonists' best interests in mind. He loudly criticized the Stamp Act of 1765 and the Townshend Acts of 1767.

Adams was not only patriotic, he was principled. He demonstrated this when he voluntarily represented the British soldiers accused of murder in the Boston Massacre of March 1770. He did this to make sure that the soldiers had a fair trial. The case ended in most of the soldiers being acquitted, or not guilty.

In 1774, Adams was one of the delegates Massachusetts sent to the First Continental Congress in Philadelphia. In 1775, he was again a delegate to the Second Continental Congress. He nominated George Washington to serve as commander of the colonial forces in the Revolutionary War. Adams would later become a congressional delegate and nominate Thomas Jefferson to draft the Declaration of Independence.

In 1778, Adams went to Paris to secure aid for the colonists' cause. The next year, he went back to America, where he served as the main framer of the Massachusetts Constitution. The Massachusetts Constitution is the world's oldest surviving written constitution. By the early 1780s, Adams was in Europe again as a diplomat. In 1783, he, John Jay, and Benjamin Franklin were helpful in negotiating the Treaty of Paris, which officially ended hostilities between America and Britain.

Adams stayed in Europe after the war, and served as the United States' first ambassador to Britain, from 1785 to 1788. After returning to America, he was part of the 1789 Constitutional Convention that nominated Washington to serve as the nation's first president. He was elected the vice-president of the

US, and he served until 1797, when he became the president.

When Adams entered office, his presidency was quickly consumed with foreign affairs. Britain and France were at war, and this directly affected America's economy. During Washington's tenure, he had managed to remain neutral. By Adams' tenure however, American merchants on the high seas were facing great difficulty. The new nation was also greatly divided into factions, some of whom supported the French, while some supported the British.

In 1797, Adams sent a group of delegates to France to arrange a treaty, but the French refused to meet with them. The French foreign minister, Charles Maurice de Talleyrand-Perigord, demanded a large bribe before agreeing to begin any negotiations. He refused to pay the bribe. This incident became known as the XYZ Affair. It annoyed the American public and made Adams more popular among the people.

The United States and France then engaged in an undeclared naval war known as the Quasi-War, which dominated the remainder of Adams's presidency. Adams led a part of the army and the navy, and the navy won several successes in the Quasi-War.

The war cost a lot of money, and Congress passed the Direct Tax Act of 1798 to generate revenue. As a result, people started to protest. One of such protests is the Fries's Rebellion. The 5th Congress then passed four bills, collectively known as the Alien and Sedition Acts. These acts made it more difficult for immigrants to become U.S. citizens. They also allowed the president to imprison and deport non-citizens deemed dangerous or who were from a hostile nation. They made it a crime to say anything that was false and critical of the federal government. The Democratic-Republican party harshly criticized the laws for being unconstitutional. The Federalist party, which Adams was a part of, argued that the bills strengthened national security during the time of conflict.

John Adams Meeting with the French Consul at President's House in Philadelphia, Pennsylvania

Many Americans, who still felt the pain of British oppression, feared that their new government might resort to similar tactics. Eventually, it made Adams unpopular with the people. When his tenure ended in 1800, he lost the election to Thomas Jefferson, his vice-president.

After his presidency, Adams had a long and productive retirement with his wife in Quincy, Massachusetts. He spent the next twenty-five years writing columns, books, and letters. In 1812, he began exchanging letters with his old rival Thomas

Jefferson, and they corresponded for the rest of their lives.

In 1824, John Adams's son, John Quincy Adams, became America's sixth president. By then, most of the other signatories to the Declaration of Independence had died. The older John Adams and Thomas Jefferson were among the last surviving signatories. On July 4, 1826 (the Declaration's 50th anniversary), the 90-year-old Adams uttered his last words: "Thomas Jefferson still survives." He died later that day. He did not know that earlier that morning, Jefferson had also passed away.

Conclusion

The time of the American Revolution was a difficult one. The pilgrims survived a difficult journey across the ocean, faced natives and famine, and still found a way to prosper. The colonists fought against their country of origin, England, and demanded their independence in the Revolutionary War. Time and time again, they faced adversity with bravery.

Because of these strong men and women, the United States was formed as a democracy, a place where people were able to believe whatever religion they chose, and a place allowing for prosperity of all. The Founding Fathers wrote the documents the country is founded on- The Declaration of Independence, the Constitution, the Articles of Confederation, and the Bill of Rights.

Founding Fathers and their brilliance created the United States and gave it the foundation it still sits on.

More from us

Visit our book store at: www.dinobibi.com

History series

Travel series

Made in the USA
Las Vegas, NV
25 August 2022

54003821R00069